stitching
Love and Kindness

14 Needlework Projects in Cross Stitch, Punch Needle Embroidery, and Sewing for Valentine's Day and Beyond

Credits

Book Design and Layout... Amanda Mae MacNaughton of Ardith Design

Cross Stitch Charting, Cross Stitch Model Stitching, Original Punch Needle Artwork, Punch Needle Model Stitching, and Model Finishing... Amanda Mae MacNaughton of Ardith Design

Proofreading and Editing.. Michelle Garrette of Bendy Stitchy Designs

Published by Ardith Design LLC. P.O. Box 1181 Mount Airy, Maryland 21771 United States of America.

ardithdesign.com #ardithdesign @ardithdesign #stitchingloveandkindness

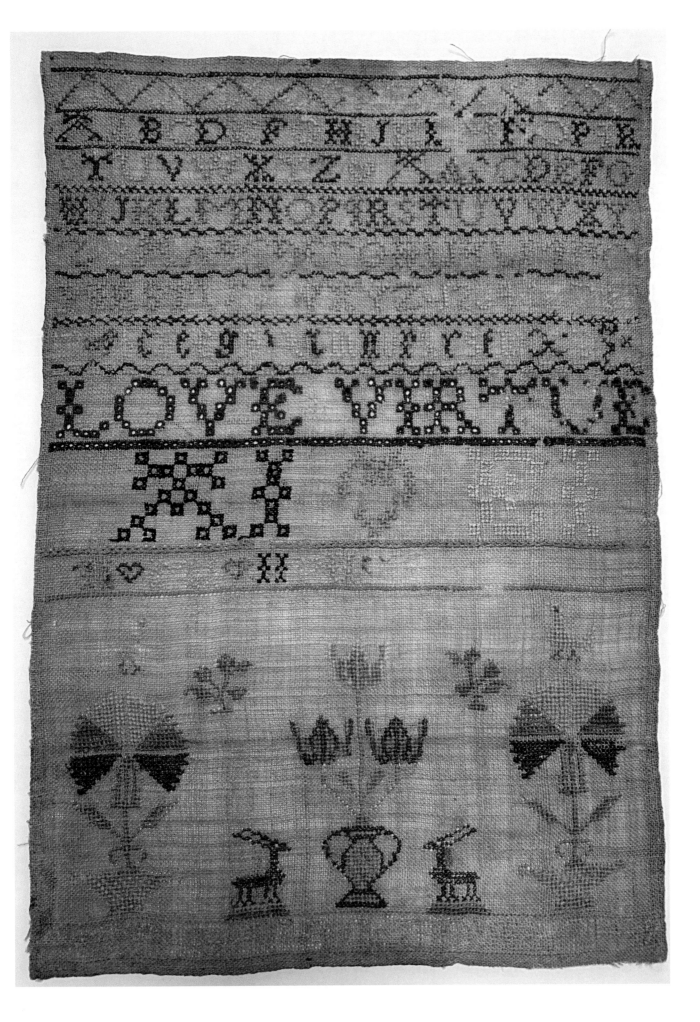

Table of Contents

Make a colored copy of this page on paper card stock. Cut out each picture along the pink border. Use a hole punch at the bottom of each picture. I used a heart shaped punch used in scrapbooking. Now place your thread on each card. You can write the floss company and number on the back of each card. Fun tip: these make excellent gift tags or miniature love notes.

Love Pug

Love Pug

40 Stitches Wide x 60 Stitches High

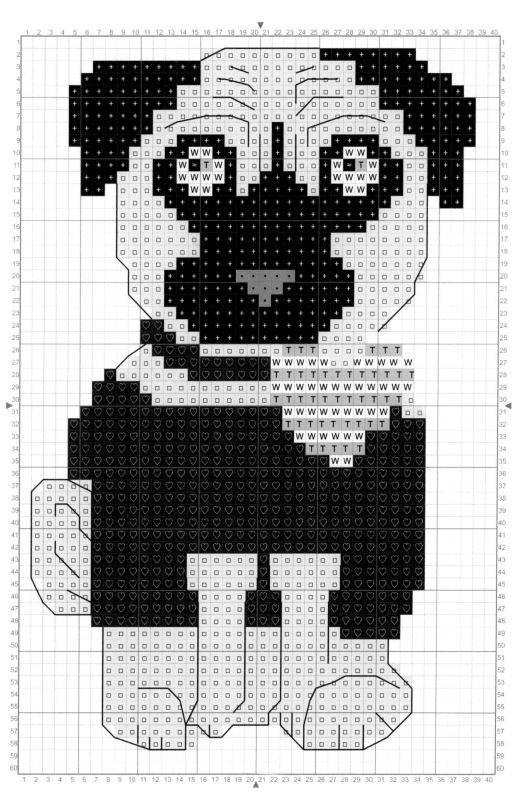

Pugs & Kisses

Symbol	DMC
+	838
□	3823
T	964
W	B5200
≈	310
•	899
♡	326
Backstitch	838

Love You

This is a counted cross-stitch pattern of a little love pug. This little fawn pug is wearing a darling red sweater to stay warm. This Love Pug is ready to cuddle for Valentine's Day. Who doesn't love to put clothes on a pug?

The model is stitched on 18 count white Aida fabric using two strands of DMC floss over one hole. The backstitching uses two strands of DMC 838.

This is finished in a four inch hoop.

Fraktur Love Birds

The model is stitched on 18 count Fiddler's cloth Aida with two strands of DMC floss over one hole.

The border of the design is stitched in DMC 498. All backstitching is done in two strands of DMC 498. The center motifs including the birds, lock, key, and hearts are stitched with DMC 4516 Black Forest thread. The eye for each bird is a colonial knot using two strands of DMC 310 black.

Fraktur Love Birds
55 Stitches Wide x108 Stitches High

Sealed with a Kiss

The model is stitched on 18 count white Aida fabric using two strands of DMC floss over one hole. This model uses four colors in full cross stitches. It is attached to an acid-free matte board. A small rare earth magnet is super glued to the back of the piece. This allows it to attach to the metal accessory.

Sealed with a Kiss

44 Stitches Wide x 64 Stitches High

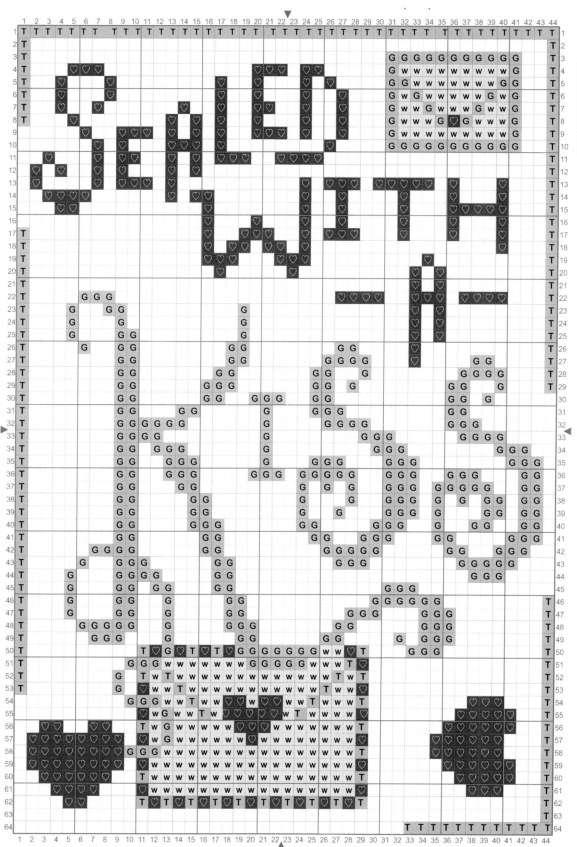

Symbol	DMC
♡	3801
w	745
T	964
G	966

Bunches of Love

Bunches of Love is a small counted cross-stitch pattern featuring a chalkboard design of a pair of carrots and the phrase, "bunches of love." Stitch this pattern up in time for spring, for a loved one, for an avid gardener, or for a person that just loves carrots!

The model is stitched on 32 count black linen with two strands of DMC floss over two linen threads. The piece is mounted on a vintage farmhouse cheese grater.

The DMC colors include DMC 13 medium light nile green, DMC 16 light chartreuse, and DMC 19 medium light autumn gold.

Bunches of Love

68 Stitches Wide x 39 Stitches High

Symbol	DMC
G	016
+	013
▽	019

Tidbits of Affection

Finished Design Size: 4.35 inches wide by 5 inches high (11 x 12.7 cm)

The model is stitched using one strand of Sulky 712-1001 Snow White 12 weight cotton petites thread. It is stitched on hand-dyed 18 count burgundy red Aida fabric. It is mounted on acid free matte board and attached to a 7.2 inch wooden box. The box is painted with two coats of Apple Barrel cream white acrylic paint. This box can hold love notes, trinkets, and tidbits. If you don't want to use a box, attach your finished stitch to a clear glass jar. The jar can hold notes of gratitude or be used as a candy jar.

Tidbits of Affection

69 Stitches Wide by 73 Stitches High

Starburst Bouquet

Finished Design Size: 2 Inches Wide by 3.25 inches High (5 cm x 8.25 cm)

Starburst Bouquet is a ultra petite cross stitch piece. It is inspired by a bouquet motif on a Netherlands Sampler at the Cleveland Museum of Art.

The model is stitched with one strand of DMC 6 strand embroidery floss over one linen thread. It is stitched on 32 count Chalkboard black linen.

The design is affixed to an acid-free matte board and glued using Aleene's Tacky Glue on a small wooden paddle made by Notforgotten Farm. The petite paddle measures 2 inches by 5 inches.

If stitching one-over-one on black linen is not your style, no worries. This would look darling on any count of fabric.

Starburst Bouquet

41 Stitches Wide x 61 Stitches High

Symbol	DMC	Name
♥	026	Hyacinth
□	024	Pale Lilac
G	016	Ivy
O	019	Terra cotta
★	013	Spearmint
▲	020	Flesh

Love and Virtue 1830 Sampler

143 Stitches Wide by 221 Stitches High

Colors

2	310
5	DMC 3813
B	DMC 3821
E	DMC 471
8	DMC 351
P	DMC 3716
◉	DMC 957
∧	DMC 834
◣	DMC 564
◩	DMC 3031
◆	DMC 676
■	DMC 816
■	DMC 814
9	DMC 948
C	DMC 3811
a	DMC 353
4	DMC 3802
★	DMC 945
■	DMC 817
◥	DMC 3822
Y	DMC 819
♣	DMC ECRUT
⬆	DMC 3346
J	DMC 300

This is such a lovely historic sampler. I purchased this sampler at an online auction in the spring of 2019. The seller of the sampler dated it circa 1830 based on its motifs and the subject matter. It measures 12 inches wide by 17.5 inches high. While it has significant thread loss, its charm and sentiment remains intact. The words, "Love" and "Virtue" are prominently stitched across the linen using a five point eyelet stitch. Using the reverse side of the needlework, I matched the wool threads to DMC six-strand cotton floss colors. I love the vibrancy of this color palette.

I have charted this sampler based on the existing state of the stitching. Many of the numbers and letters are missing. Use your discretion if you would like to add your own initials, numbers, or letters to the blank spaces in the chart. The bottom of the sampler below the stags is a row of missing stitches. Fill this space in with an anniversary date or wedding date.

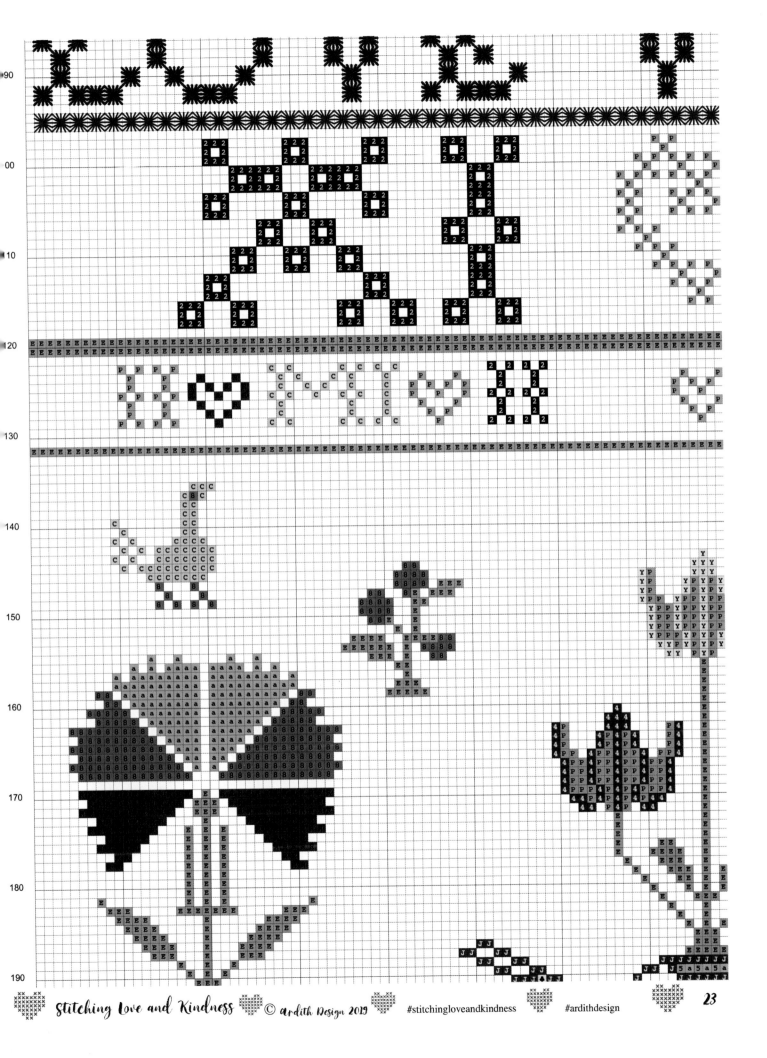

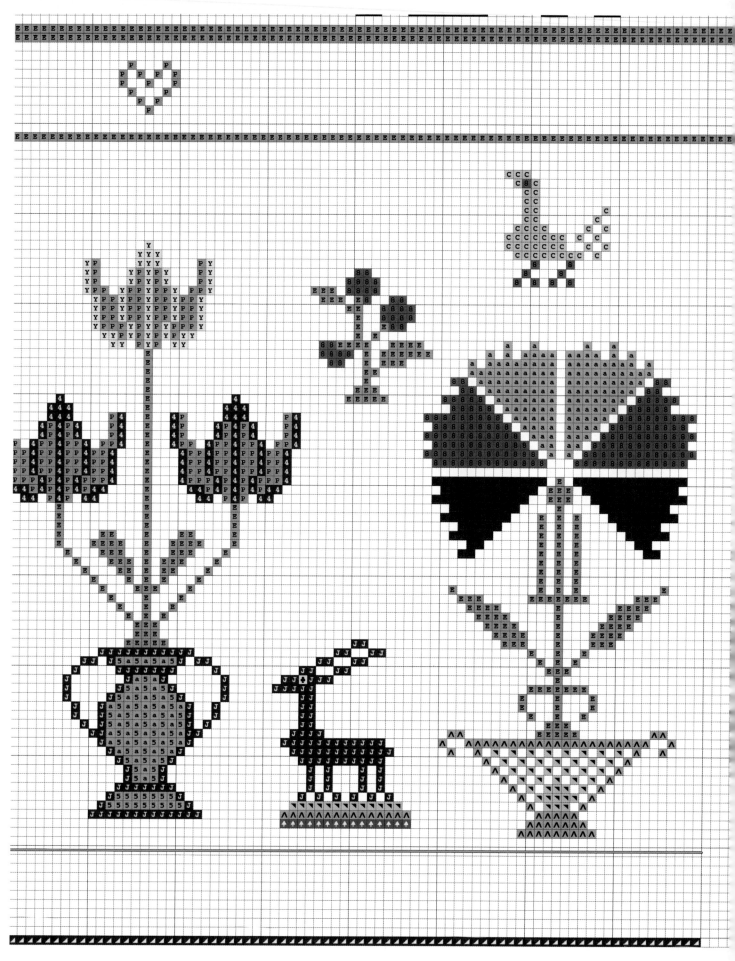

Love and Virtue 1830 Sampler
Floss List & Color Key

	Number		Name:	Strands	Length	Stitches
2	310		DMC	1	9.68 yd.	492
5	DMC	3813	Blue Green light	2	1.54 yd.	60
B	DMC	3821	Straw	2	0.53 yd.	27
E	DMC	471	Avocado Green very lt	2	21.67 yd.	1102
8	DMC	351	Coral	2	10.31 yd.	524
P	DMC	3716	Dusty Rose very light	2	5.90 yd.	300
◉	DMC	957	Geranium pale	2	4.52 yd.	230
Λ	DMC	834	Golden Olive very light	2	11.92 yd.	606
◣	DMC	564	Jade very light	2	2.81 yd.	143
◿	DMC	3031	Mocha Brown very dark	2	29.45 yd.	1324
◆	DMC	676	Old Gold light	2	2.10 yd.	107
■	DMC	816	Garnet	2	11.88 yd.	233
■	DMC	814	Garnet dark	2	4.25 yd.	216
9	DMC	948	Peach very light	2	2.79 yd.	142
C	DMC	3811	Turquoise very light	2	2.71 yd.	138
a	DMC	353	Peach	2	6.47 yd.	329
4	DMC	3802	Antique Mauve very dk	2	2.20 yd.	112
★	DMC	945	Tawny medium	2	0.37 yd.	19
■	DMC	817	Coral Red very dark	2	7.93 yd.	403
◥	DMC	3822	Straw light	2	2.05 yd.	104
Y	DMC	819	Baby Pink light	2	1.10 yd.	56
♣	DMC	ECRUT	Ecru	2	0.04 yd.	2
⬆	DMC	3346	Hunter Green	2	0.59 yd.	30
J	DMC	300	Mahogany very dark	2	5.19 yd.	264

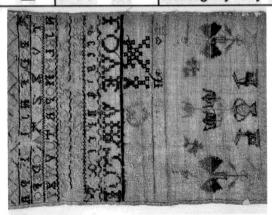

Made with Love Envelope

Supplies

- Envelope Panel* by Ardith Design

- Glass seed beads size 8 to blanket stitch down the side seams of the envelope

- Carnation flower patch stitched from the Love and Virtue Sampler in DMC 601, DMC 604 DMC 605

- Pellon 44F fusible interfacing

- Coordinating pink thread

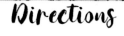

Directions

Cut out the fabric panel, fold down the dark pink edges, and iron them to create the ¼ inch inseam. With your sewing machine, sew down all the way around the edges of the panel. Next fold the panel in half to create the envelope. With your needle and thread, create a blanket stitch down the two sides of the envelope. There is a cream white and pink checkerboard pattern on each border that acts as a guide for each blanket stitch. If you choose, attach a size 8 glass seed bead as you alternate between a blanket stitch with a bead and one without a bead. Now your envelope is ready to use! If you like, you can add a fun carnation flower patch.

* The envelope fabric panel is available as a fat quarter in Linen Cotton Canvas at the ardith_design shop on Spoonflower. The fat quarter comes with two needle book panels and two envelope panels. Stitch up a set for you and and a set for a loved one.

Made with Love Envelope Patch

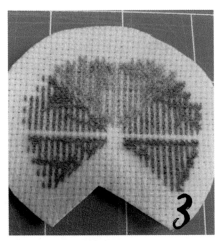

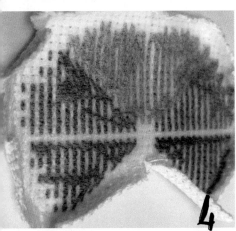

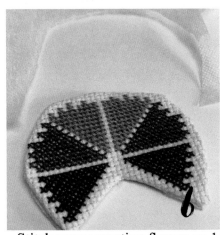

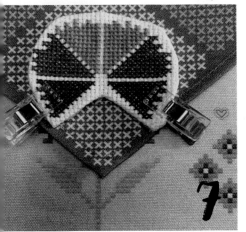

1.   Stitch your carnation flower on 14 count white Aida fabric. Cut out interfacing the same size as your finished stitch.

2.   Iron down interfacing.

3.   Cut out around the design leaving enough space to fold over and iron down the edges.

4.   With your scissors, make small snips around the corners and fold over the edges. Iron it down again.

5. Cut out another piece of interfacing matching your flower shape. It needs to be the exact layout of your flower. Iron down the interfacing over the folded over edges. This step secures the Aida fabric down to the back of the piece. You can repeat this step again for extra stability or thickness to your patch.

6.   Your flower patch should be ready to sew down to your envelope.

7.   Pin down or clip your patch in place. Thread an embroidery needle with white or cream thread that will blend into the white Aida fabric. Hand stitch your patch in place.

8. Now admire your handiwork: sewn envelope, cross stitch patch, and beadwork.

 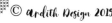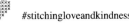

Basket of Hearts
in Colonial Knots

Colors

- **DMC 677** Very Light Old Gold

- **DMC 830** Dark Golden Olive Green

- **DMC 831** Medium Golden Olive Green

- **DMC 739** Very Light Tan Brown

- **DMC 783** Medium Topaz Brown

- **DMC 815** Medium Garnet Red

- **DMC 816** Garnet Red

- **DMC 918** Dark Copper Red

Basket of Hearts is composed entirely of colonial knots. The model is stitched on 36 count Dill green Edinburgh linen by Picture this Plus. Charted as a cross stitch piece, each knot is placed over two strands of linen thread (similar to adding a full cross stitch in its place). After you finish a segment, go back and fill in any areas of bare linen. The more knots you make, the thicker and fuller each piece will look. For instance, you can add more knots in the hearts, but leave space between the knots on the green stems. The piece uses three strands of DMC embroidery floss. The model is stretched and mounted on 4 x 6 inch acid-free matte board. The piece is placed on a wooden heart wall hanging by Notforgotten Farm.

Basket of Hearts

G	DMC	677
▼	DMC	830
★	DMC	831
T	DMC	739
♣	DMC	783
■	DMC	815
■	DMC	816
■	DMC	918

Punch Needle Directions

- Trace the pattern onto weavers cloth using a thin tip permanent marker. I use the black Sharpie 0.8mm Stylo Pen. The patterns are in this book are ready to trace directly onto your weavers cloth.

- Use setting number one (#1) on your Ultra Punch.

- Install the small needle that comes with your Ultra Punch in order to use a single strand of Sulky 12 weight cotton petites thread.

- For the three designs in this book, use one strand of Sulky 12 weight cotton petites thread. Start punching the small details first and leave the background until the end to punch.

- When your design is finished, cut out along the edge of the weavers cloth.

- Using a paint brush, I added a layer of Aleene's Tacky Glue to the back of the piece. I folded over the extra fabric and glued it down. I allowed the glue to completely dry before I fully finished each project.

Punch Needle Bouquet

Finished Design Size 2 inches x 3.25 inches (5 cm x 8.25 cm)

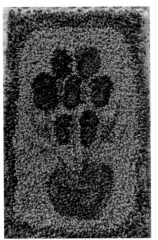

Colors

- **Sulky 712-4042, Redwork**: Red outline on each flower.

- **Sulky 712-4020, Moss Melody:** The green leaves and stem

- **Sulky 712-4056, Periwinkles:** Blue flower vase and blue geometric border

- **Sulky 712-0562, Spice:** Background

- **Sulky 712-1303, Watermelon:** Pink center of each flower

Finishing

Attached to a 2 x 5 inch small wooden paddle by Notforgotten Farm. The punch needle is glued down along with a cotton lace trim border using Aleene's Tacky Glue.

Punch Needle Gnome

Finished Design Size: 2.5 inch diameter circle (6.35 cm)

Colors

- **Sulky 712-1039, True Red:** Hearts and hat

- **Sulky 712-1234, Almost Black:** Eyes

- **Sulky 712-1225, Pastel Pink:** Cheeks, hat band, heart outline

- **Sulky 712-1015 Medium Peach:** Skin

- **Sulky 712-1058 Tawny Brown:** Nose and hair

- **Sulky 712-4001 Parchment:** Background

Finishing

The punch needle is glued down to a wood round using Aleene's Tacky Glue. On the back of the first wood round, attach a red ribbon loop to act as a hanger. Next, hot glue a second wood round down to hide the back of the ribbon. Using your tacky glue, attach a small red ribbon along the design's perimeter to hide the weavers cloth that might peak through the side.

Punch Needle Love You

Finished Design Size: Circle with a 3 inch diameter (7.6 cm)

Colors

- **Sulky 712-4030, Antique Rose:** The words "Love You" and the heart. Setting No. 2 on your Ultra Punch.

- **Sulky 712-1225, Pastel Pink:** Background. Setting No. 1 on your Ultra Punch. Please note that there is enough thread on one spool to finish the 3 inch circle. If you wish to make this design larger, you will need an additional spool to complete the design.

Finishing

The punch needle is glued down to a wooden heart ornament along with a coordinating pink pom pom trim.

Love Kindness Empathy
an Adaptation Sampler

161 Stitches Wide by 115 Stitches High

This is an adaptation sampler based on a bottom segment of the Love and Virtue 1830 Sampler featured in this book. Some subtle changes to the placement of the motifs and the new lettering, "love, kindness, empathy" differentiate it from the original sampler. The most striking difference to this adaptation sampler, however, is the color palette. I brightened up the colors and added a DMC Coloris variegated thread. DMC 4502 Camelia incorporates green, blue, pink. Make sure you complete each cross stitch when you are stitching with DMC 4502 because the colors change so quickly as you are stitching.

The model is stitched on a 32 count Soft Porcelain Linen by Luminous Fiber Arts. It is stitched with two strands of floss over two linen threads. The top of the carnation flowers are stitched with a blend of DMC 3770 and DMC 602. The flower urns are stitched with DMC 4502. Depending on where you start with your strand of floss, your urn could have more pinks or more green and blue tones as you stitch. This is why the urns on the model look so different from each other.

Feel free to choose your own color palette and stitch this delightful sampler. The central message of this piece is to spread love, kindness, and empathy.

Love Kindness Empathy Sampler

Floss List & Color Key

	Number	Name:	Strands	Length	Stitches
G	DMC 3348	Yellow Green light	2	10.36 yd.	527
★	GAS 0780	Hibiscus	2	20.91 yd.	1063
4	DMC 712	Cream	2	4.41 yd.	224
E	DMC 783	Topaz medium	2	5.57 yd.	283
●	DMC 3770 [+] DMC 602	Very light tawny brown and medium cranberry pink	2	5.66 yd.	288
P	DMC 3325	Baby Blue light	2	2.87 yd.	146
■	DMC 600	Cranberry very dark	2	7.51 yd.	382
Λ	DMC 772	Yellow Green very light	2	5.41 yd.	275
■	DMC 4502	Camelia DMC Coloris	2	19.77 yd.	1005
◆	DMC 605	Cranberry very light	2	1.53 yd.	78
C	DMC 604	Cranberry light	2	1.69 yd.	86

KINDNESS

EMPATHY

Needle Book

Sew up this is a darling cross stitch inspired needle book

Supplies

- Needle Book Panel* by Ardith Design

- 4.5 x 8.5 inch (11.4 x 21.6 cm) piece of coordinating quilting cotton fabric

- 3.75 inch x 7.75 inch (9.5 x 19.7 cm) Pellon 44F fabric interfacing to iron onto the quilting cotton to add extra reinforcement to the book.

- 8 x 8 inch (20.3 cm) square of cream white Weeks Dye Works wool. This piece will be cut into two 3.5 inch x 7 inch (8.9 cm x 17.8 cm) pieces

- 1 yard of ribbon. I used a vintage red silk ribbon and knotted the ends. You will cut the ribbon into two 18 inch pieces.

- Sulky 712-4042 thread, two strands used to hand stitch the wool pieces to the quilting cotton.

using quilting cotton for both sides of the needle book.

3.75 inch x 7.75 inch template to cut out wool for the pages of the needle book. Cut two (2)

4.5 x 8.5 Inch template for the front and back of the needle book. Cut two (2) if you do not have the fabric panel and you are

3.75 inch x 7.75 inch template

4.5 x 8.5 Inch template

* Needle book fabric panel is available as a fat quarter in Linen Cotton Canvas at the ardith_design shop on Spoonflower. The fat quarter comes with two needle book panels and two envelope panels. Stitch up a set for you and and a set for a loved one.

Needle Book Directions

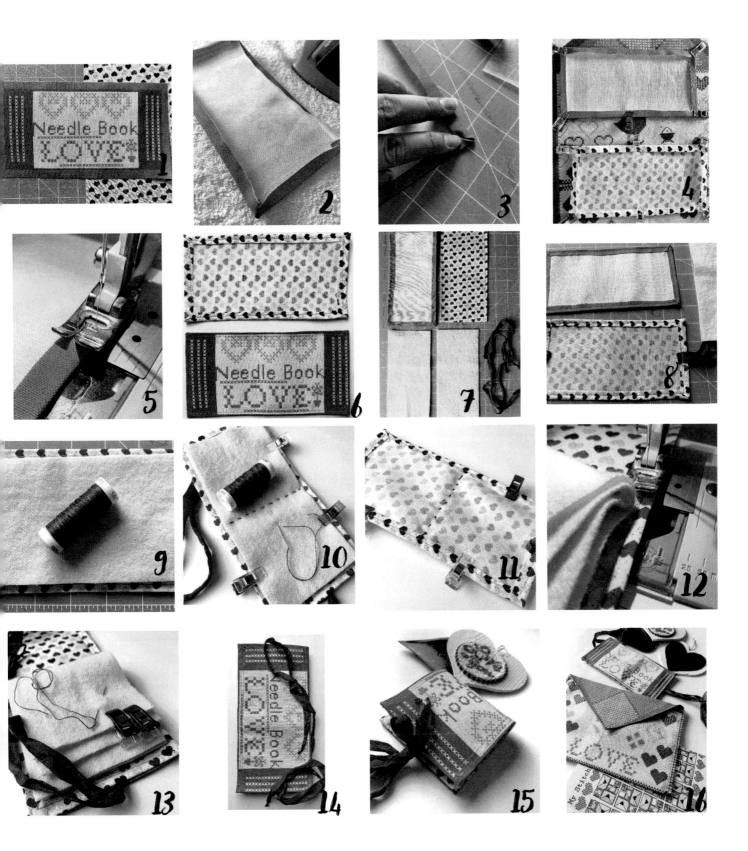

Needle Book Directions
Directions

1. Cut out the needle book panel and the coordinating quilting cotton. Iron on the interfacing.

2. Fold over the light pink edges of the panel and press. Iron down all edges.

3. Fold the corners and press with the hot iron.

4. Clip or pin down all edges and prep to sew the border down with a ¼ inch seam allowance.

5. Sew down all sides of the panel and the quilting cotton.

6. Finish sewing all sides. Trim all excess threads off. Press with your iron again.

7. Cut the two pieces of wool to 3.5 x 7 inches. Your ribbon should be two 18 inch pieces.

8. Secure the ribbon to the center on both sides of the quilting cotton.

9. Flip the quilting cotton with the print facing up. Arrange the two wool pieces in the center of the fabric. Prep a embroidery size 11 needle and thread to hand stitch the wool down through the center. I used two strands of Sulky 712-4042.

10. Clip down and secure the pieces and hand stitch the pieces together.

11. Flip over and secure the hand stitched thread.

12. Place the backsides of the needle book panel and the quilting cotton together and sew them together. Please be careful of the wool and the ribbon.

13. The two sections should now be sewn together. The ribbon should be secure between the two fabric pieces. The wool interior is now ready to hold your needles and sewing clips.

14. Here is the front of my Needle Book. My kids helped me at the sewing machine, which resulted in wonky stitching. I think that adds character and a great memory. I have wonky stitches and that's okay.

15. The needle book folds up and secures with the ribbon. I knotted the ribbon ends. You can always add large beads to the ends for extra decoration.

16. Your needle book is now ready to use. Enjoy!

Resources

- Original art and cross stitch designs available at ardithdesign.com

- Needle Book and Cross Stitch Valentine Envelope fat quarter fabric panel in cotton canvas by Ardith Design. Order a fat quarter, https://www.spoonflower.com/profiles/ardith_design

- My Stitching Friends: Address Book for my Needlework Friends and Social Media Contacts by Ardith Design is available on Amazon https://amzn.to/2PDNMwU

- Soft Porcelain Linen by Luminous Fiber Arts. www.etsy.com/shop/LuminousFiberArts

- Sulky 12 Weight Cotton Petites Thread, Sulky of America. www.sulky.com

- Miniature Wooden Paddle and Heart Wall Hanging, Notforgotten Farm. www.notforgottenfarm.etsy.com

- Ultra Punch Needle, ceramic thread holder, weavers cloth, and Gentle Art Sampler Threads can be purchased at Primitive Homespuns Wool and Needleworks, www.phwoolandneedle.com

- The Bee CompanyWooden Heart Buttons (Item Number TB3CR. SKU 664149379815) and 36 count Dill Linen by Picture This Plus purchased at www.kittenstitcher.com

- Unfinished Wood Box for "Tidbits of Affection," Michaels Craft Store. ArtMinds Box. Item #357778. SKU 652695556517

- Pellon 44F fabric interfacing at your local quilt shop.

- DMC 6 Strand Embroidery Floss www.dmc.com

- A special thank you to Kathy Makers at Primitive Homespuns for teaching me Punch Needle Embroidery. Take a class at Primitive Homespuns and explore historic Frederick, Maryland.

- Thank you to Michelle Garrette for her feedback and editing assistance, https://bendystitchydesigns.com

Happy Stitching

Made in the USA
Middletown, DE
27 December 2020